Passive Income Ideas 2023

Discover the Best Work From Home Business Ideas to Build Passive Income and Quit Your 9-5

Wayne Peters

© **Copyright 2023 - All rights reserved.**

The content contained within this book may not be reproduced, duplicated, or transmitted without direct written permission from the author or the publisher.

Under no circumstances will any blame or legal responsibility be held against the publisher, or author, for any damages, reparation, or monetary loss due to the information contained within this book, either directly or indirectly.

Legal Notice:

This book is copyright protected. It is only for personal use. You cannot amend, distribute, sell, use, quote or paraphrase any part, or the content within this book, without the consent of the author or publisher.

Disclaimer Notice:

Please note the information contained within this document is for educational and entertainment purposes only. All effort has been executed to present accurate, up to date, reliable, complete information. No warranties of any kind are declared or implied. Readers acknowledge that the author is not engaged in the rendering of legal, financial, medical or professional advice. The content within this book has been derived from various sources. Please consult a licensed professional before attempting any techniques outlined in this book.

By reading this document, the reader agrees that under no circumstances is the author responsible for any losses, direct or indirect, that are incurred as a result of the use of the information contained within this document, including, but not limited to, errors, omissions, or inaccuracies.

Table of Contents

INTRODUCTION 1

CHAPTER 1: PERFORMANCE-BASED AFFILIATE MARKETING ... 5

   How It Works 6
   What You Need 8
   How to Get Started 9
      Select a Niche 9
      Build an Audience 10
      Choose Your Affiliate Program 11
      Create Content 13
      Receive Commissions 14
   Action Steps 14

CHAPTER 2: START A PROFITABLE BLOG 17

   How It Works 17
   What You Need 19
   How to Get Started 21
      Choose Your Platform 21
      Sort out Your SEO 22
      Build Your Blog Library 24
      Join an Advertising Network 24
   Action Steps 25

CHAPTER 3: GROW YOUR YOUTUBE CHANNEL 27

   How It Works 27
   What You Need 28
   How to Get Started 29
      Create and Optimize Your Channel 29
      Record and Upload Regular Videos 31
      Monetize Your Channel 33
   Action Steps 35

CHAPTER 4: DROPSHIPPING PHYSICAL PRODUCTS 37

How It Works 37
What You Need 38
How to Get Started 39
    Market and Product Research 39
    Set Up Your Store 41
    Promote Your Products 43
Action Steps 44

CHAPTER 5: ATTRACTIVE DIGITAL PRODUCTS THAT SELL 47

How It Works 47
What You Need 48
How to Get Started 49
    Product Research 49
    Create Your Digital Product 51
    Diversify Your Product Suite 52
    Marketplaces Versus Your Own Website 53
    Creating a Ready-To-Buy Audience 55
Action Steps 56

CHAPTER 6: CREATE YOUR OWN COURSE 59

How It Works 59
How to Get Started 61
    Creating Your Course 61
    Where to Host Your Course 65
    Marketing Your Course 67
Actions Steps 69

CONCLUSION 71

REFERENCES 75

Introduction

How would it feel to have more time freedom in your day to day life? More time for your family and friends, more time to pursue hobbies—and none of the restrictions that come with a demanding 9-to-5 job?

There is only so much time in a day and working more hours means less control over your own life and how you spend your personal time. The harsh reality is that living costs continue to grow, and it is getting to the point when one job may not be enough anymore. As expenses increase, your income may not, which may result in the need to find a second—or even third—job. Working harder does not necessarily guarantee more income when you're working under the strict regulations and structures of a full time job.

That's where *passive income* comes in, as a solution to salaries that don't grow fast enough to keep up with daily expenses. Passive income allows you the freedom and independence to make money on your own time. You can begin to build a business on your own terms that benefits you and your unique needs. But what is passive income?

Passive income differs from active income as you are able to set it up once and continue earning money as opposed to being paid based on consistent output. This consistent output is active income, which refers to being paid by the hour, earning a salary, and even freelance work. You're putting in your time and energy on a consistent basis to earn a living.

In today's world that is not as sustainable anymore as it was. People are feeling overworked and suffering from burnout.

Passive income on the other hand allows you to earn money while you're not necessarily working. The money you earn is thus not directly related to the amount of hours you put in. Replacing your income with passive income may take time in the beginning, but once you put in the work to create a passive income revenue stream you will reap the rewards even after you've stopped working on them! The best part? Passive income doesn't have a limit. With a salary there is only so much you can earn but passive income can continue to grow.

There are a myriad of ways to create passive income but not all of them are cost-effective and some may even require a specific skill set.

In this book we'll be going over six ways that you can start generating passive income without the need for specialized skills and without breaking the bank. These methods complement one another well, meaning that you can slowly combine a few of these methods to bring in more money from different avenues. This results in a more sustainable way of working that will benefit you long term.

The six types of passive income outlined in this book are ideal for beginners—all you need is internet access and you're good to go! First, we'll look at affiliate marketing, which once you understand, will tie in nicely with other methods of passive income, such as starting a profitable blog, and growing your YouTube channel. Having a blog and a YouTube channel are both an excellent way to put yourself out there and grow an audience that will be more likely to purchase your passive income products that we'll cover later in the book. We'll go into more detail about creating a blog and YouTube channel in Chapters 2 and 3 respectively. The key to these two methods is *content*!

In Chapter 4 you'll be introduced to the concept of 'dropshipping' and the opportunities that this more physical approach to passive income possesses. It may be an unfamiliar term but it is much simpler than it sounds! Next, we'll explore digital products that you can start selling on different marketplaces to boost your passive income. Digital products can be as simple as creating and selling ebooks on Amazon. Finally, we'll look at creating online courses—whether they be long courses that take the student on a journey or short mini courses that add on-the-go actionable value. This method can be made easy if you have content on your blog and YouTube channel thanks to the concept of content repurposing.

Together, these six avenues can create a profitable business that will grow from a side hustle into the opportunity to quit your 9-to-5 job. They complement one another perfectly in a way that will make it easier for you to utilize each to generate more passive income.

At the end of the day one method of passive income doesn't exist in isolation because selecting a few options will boost your chance of success. At its core this book is here to show you how these particular forms of passive income can offer you time freedom while being easy and cost-effective to implement.

Chapter 1:

Performance-Based Affiliate Marketing

Affiliate marketing is a method of passive income that is usually offered by merchants or entrepreneurs that create a product or service. The merchant offers commissions to people or shares a portion of revenue with these affiliates (in this case it would be you) in order to gain transactions. Originally affiliate marketing came about for online stores to drive sales on their website, but today your favorite online tools and content creators may offer affiliate programs too. The way that it works involves you receiving a unique affiliate link from the merchant that you can share with your own audience. If your audience purchases a product from the online store using your affiliate link, you receive a monetary reward as a result of their purchase. This could be either commissions based on a percentage of sales, or fixed rates that are determined by the service provider for each purchase of a product or service.

It's a form of performance-based passive income as it is dependent on whether or not people buy the product using your affiliate link. Your affiliate link is a trackable link that contains a code unique to you that the merchant uses to accurately determine conversions or sales that are generated through the use of your link. Another option, aside from a link containing a unique code, is a coupon code linked to you that customers can use when buying a product or service. This personalized coupon code will help to track the sales that are being made as a result of your promotion of those products or services.

The upside to affiliate marketing is that you're promoting other companies' or entrepreneurs' products, meaning less work for you if you're not wanting to create your own products to sell (which we'll cover in Chapter 6). You're simply promoting their products in exchange for a commission with no inconvenience to you, as you don't need to be involved in the product delivery process at all! All you need to do is create content that promotes the products you choose to endorse and share that across your platforms to encourage conversions that will increase your passive income earnings.

How It Works

There are a few models to keep in mind when it comes to affiliate marketing and how you will be rewarded based on the sales you make. The first is *pay-per-click (PPC)*, which results in the affiliate being paid based on the number of clicks that their unique link receives. The second model is *pay-per-lead (PPL)* where the affiliate receives a commission based on leads generated such as a form submission on the merchant's website. The third affiliate model is *pay-per-sale (PPS)*, which is the most common form of affiliate marketing—and most likely what you would encounter when joining an affiliate program to earn passive income. This method involves receiving a commission for any sale that you're able to generate with the use of your unique link.

When getting into affiliate marketing you can choose to promote a merchant or join an affiliate network. You can do both although each option has its own advantages and disadvantages. If you join the affiliate programs of specific merchants, you may be using different software each time in order to manage your affiliate information. You may need to get familiar with the platform but once you click around and learn how it works it will be very easy to manage. This can be tricky to manage although creating a helpful spreadsheet to keep track of your affiliate information can save you a lot of time. Merchants can be established companies or individuals giving you a lot of options in terms of who you would like to be an affiliate for. On the other hand, if you join an affiliate network, such as ShareASale or ClickBank, you'll have the option to manage all of your affiliate marketing programs in one place. These affiliate networks bridge the gap between you, as the affiliate, and the merchant, in order to manage the relationship and act as a central port of communication for both parties. This helps to establish trust and offers ease of use with all-in-one tracking, helpful reporting, and payment management.

What You Need

The best part about affiliate marketing is that it's completely free. Plus you get to promote products or services that you love using and get a reward for doing so. Affiliate marketing is a preferred way of advertising as it is cost-effective for the merchants because they only need to pay when they make a conversion. This means that there are many products and services to choose from when you're looking to utilize affiliate marketing. Due to its profitability, affiliate marketing is only growing in popularity making it an excellent passive income avenue to start using.

Growing an audience is helpful when it comes to affiliate marketing so that more people will see your link and click through to buy. This is where a blog or YouTube channel would come in as a way to maximize your exposure and increase your chances of making a sale.

Affiliate marketing is built on your credibility. If your audience knows, likes, and trusts you, they are more likely to click on your affiliate links and purchase the product or service that you are affiliated with. This means that although it may be tempting to join a lot of affiliate programs, it's important to be selective and ensure that the product you are promoting is of high quality and will only boost your credibility. If you're an expert in a particular field then it's helpful to choose affiliate programs that are relevant to that niche. Your audience will relate better to them, as they are attracted to you based on your expertise and will readily trust your recommendation.

How to Get Started

The first place to start when it comes to affiliate marketing is to have a platform that you will use to promote the products or services you want to earn a commision on. A good place to host your affiliate marketing efforts would be a website or blog, however social media platforms can work in your favor too. You need people to see the products you're promoting, which is where having an audience comes in.

Select a Niche

In order to grow your influence in the online space so that you can get eyes on your affiliate links, choose a niche or area of expertise that you can hone in on. By choosing a niche you'll be able to speak directly to the people that would be interested in the product or service that you're promoting. For example, if you have a passion for health and fitness, you could create a platform that speaks to these core values and attracts like minded people to connect with you and explore what you're offering them. We'll go into more detail on how to set up a blog or start a YouTube channel to grow influence in Chapters 2 and 3.

In the meantime, start brainstorming what area of expertise you could offer and which affiliate programs you'd like to join that complements that niche. Don't be limited by your own expertise when choosing a niche. A niche could be completely unrelated to your experience, but if it's a subject you're interested in, you're bound to enjoy learning more about it and won't tire of the subject as easily. However, do consider if there is enough that you can share about in your chosen niche. If it's too specific you may struggle to create content around it, or even find enough people who are interested.

Build an Audience

Once you've selected your platform and niche, you can begin building an audience. This may sound intimidating but if you get really clear on your target audience and who it is that you want to be speaking to it shouldn't take too long to establish an audience base.

A few ways to discover who your target audience may be is to look at other social media accounts or websites that cover topics in your niche to see who is engaging with that content. Once you've collected that information you will have a clearer idea about who you need to be speaking to. Another way to do this is by simply asking around in places your audience may be present in, such as various social media platforms, to gauge interest in your niche and what kind of content this audience would like to see from you. Content is key when it comes to promoting your affiliate offers and encouraging sales from those that engage with you. The people that read and engage with your content are the people that are more likely to buy what you're promoting as you're showcasing the value these products and services can offer them. These trusted recommendations will in turn help you earn passive income from affiliate marketing. There are numerous different ways to create content that will engage your audience and inspire them to take action. This could be in the form of social media posts that speak directly to your target audience or more personalized emails that connect with your audience. If you offer your audience quality content that they resonate with on a regular basis, they will be more primed and ready to buy your recommendations through your unique affiliate link.

Choose Your Affiliate Program

Through building relationships and connections with your chosen audience you'll be able to join affiliate programs that suit both your niche and your target audience. We've mentioned a few platforms already, such as ShareASale and ClickBank, but one of the easiest affiliate programs to get started with is Amazon Associates.

Due to the wide range of products that Amazon offers on their website, you can select the most relevant recommendations for your audience. Their affiliate marketing program has customized linking tools to enable you to use your unique affiliate link in your content. There is the opportunity to earn approximately 10% in commission when you assist with the sale of products you choose to recommend (Amazon Associates, n.d.). Joining an affiliate program does not involve any costs but if you choose to use advertisements to promote your affiliate products, the price may vary from platform to platform.

There is a right way and a wrong way to approach affiliate marketing. The wrong way to do it is to promote any and all products, regardless of whether or not you have tried them yourself. It is also not a good idea to constantly be selling to your audience. You may want people to buy your affiliate products in order to start making money but if you overwhelm them with salesy messages you may lose trust and credibility. Especially if you're promoting products that aren't of a high quality or of value to your audience. It's also important to be transparent about the fact that you'll be earning a commission if people purchase the product or service using your affiliate link. Affiliate marketing only works if you prove yourself as a credible source, and overly promoting bad products at the expense of your reputation won't work.

The best way to approach affiliate marketing is to only promote products that you have tried yourself and can genuinely recommend to your audience. This will ensure that your reputation stays intact and your audience will be more likely to purchase other products and services you recommend in the future. The best way to promote affiliate products is to show your audience how you use them personally and in a context that is relevant to your niche. A few easy ways to ensure that you're choosing the right products to endorse are: keep your audience in mind, and whether or not they will find it valuable; ensure that the product is of a high quality and that your audience will get good value for money; and double check that endorsing these products will actually lead you to earning a profitable amount of commission.

Can you think of any products that you could start promoting that fit those criteria?

Create Content

When you've joined an affiliate program you'll be able to create content around these products or services. There are so many different ways to create and share content! You could create a blog, start a YouTube channel, use email marketing, or simply post to social media to drive attention to your affiliate links and products. A few examples of ways to do this—while retaining your credibility and sharing value—are to share blog posts showcasing your favorite product recommendations or even interviewing others that enjoy these products to get a wide range of differing opinions and experiences that enlighten your audience.

Driving traffic to your affiliate products is key to making passive income from them. Another good way of doing this is by offering free value that your audience couldn't possibly say no to. This could be as simple as offering a free ebook to get them onto your email list. Once you've created this awareness and have them on your email list you can begin to nurture them with more value that leads back to your affiliate products.

Receive Commissions

You'll be able to track your affiliate marketing progress on the platform you've selected in order to see how your affiliate links are performing. This valuable insight will help you to see how you can improve and ensure more sales and passive income in the future. It's important to make sure that you're creating content that resonates with your audience in order to effectively promote your affiliate products and services.

How you get paid will depend on the program you join, as some pay commissions on a monthly or weekly basis based on how many sales or leads you've generated. It's important to be aware of how you get paid to make sure that the affiliate program you join meets the goals you have to earn passive income. For example, if you're using paid ads to promote your affiliate links you want to be sure that you're earning enough regular passive income from affiliate marketing to cover these expenses. Some affiliates can earn over $100,000 each month (Lee, 2021). However, these kinds of numbers do take time as you need to grow your audience and credibility online—but the hard work will definitely pay off!

Action Steps

Now that you have a better idea of how to get started with affiliate marketing, we've outlined what you need to do right now to get started:

1. Select your profitable niche.
2. Determine the platform you will use to enter your chosen niche.
3. Identify your target audience.
4. Start growing your audience by posting regular content.
5. Choose your affiliate program keeping in mind payment structures.
6. Tweak and adjust your content to ensure your affiliate marketing strategy is optimized.
7. Receive commissions!

Chapter 2:

Start a Profitable Blog

Blogging is part of the content marketing world. This means that you create content that's valuable in a way that inspires, educates, or entertains your target audience. Creating this type of free content is an organic way to grow your target audience by offering value to build your credibility online. However, it's important to remember that your blog content should have a purpose. This could be to get your audience to purchase products through your affiliate link (which we discussed in Chapter 1) or to purchase your own products or online courses, which we'll go into more detail about in Chapters 5 and 6. Another way to earn passive income with your blog is through display advertising.

How It Works

There are a few ways to monetize your blog, but we're going to look at display advertising in this chapter to give you an idea of how you can earn money with your blog alone. Display ads appear on your blog as either static graphic displays, pop ups that attract the attention of site visitors, or native ads—which are more integrated into your blog and quite similar to that of sponsored content.

There are two payment models that exist for display advertisements. The first is the *pay-per-click (PPC)* model that results in payment when a visitor to your site clicks on one of the display ads. PPC ads can earn you a higher commission, however it is becoming more difficult to get visitors to click on display ads due to the sheer number that appear online. The second model is *pay-per-impression (PPI)*, which means that you earn passive income whenever a visitor to your site sees an ad.

The easiest way to get ads on your site is to join an advertising network. An advertising network is a company that distributes ads on host websites on the behalf of advertisers. The network that you choose to partner with will in turn pay you based on how many clicks or impressions the ads get on your website. It's important to choose a credible advertising network as they decide which ads will be placed on your website. You definitely don't want to put off visitors to your site with ads that contain spam or unsavory content.

A popular advertising network that many bloggers use is Google AdSense. This uses the PPC payment model, and gives bloggers that display ads on their site 68% of the profits earned as a result of each click an ad gets, making it an excellent choice to start earning passive income from your blog (Juviler, 2020). However, there are a few points to keep in mind before choosing Google AdSense as your advertising network. Networks like this require a collection of blog posts already published on your site that are of a high quality. They may also require a minimum number of traffic on your site each month and high traffic to your blog is key if you want to earn a sizable amount of passive income from your blog alone.

If you're starting a blog from scratch it can be helpful to blog as often as you can to build up your library of content and increase your traffic in order to qualify for an advertising network. It's important to keep in mind that too many ads on your site can be off-putting to site visitors and damage your credibility as a blogger. Another risk is the increased use of ad blockers, or people simply ignoring advertisements when they visit a site due to the large number of ads they see on a daily basis. Don't be disheartened if this seems difficult, it is still a great option for passive income and as your blog grows you'll start to earn more passive income from it. Remember that with the help of search engine optimization (SEO), your blog posts—even the ones from a few years ago—will be visited, with the chance of visitors clicking on an ad, helping you earn passive income for a long while to come.

What You Need

There are two ways to go about creating a blog: the free way, and the paid way. You can easily create a free blog website using a content management system like *WordPress*, but the downside to this is that your URL will include the term 'wordpress' or whichever other blogging tool you choose to use as opposed to being your own unique website link. This can be a good place to start if you're not looking to spend money right away. One of the benefits is that you can experiment with the platform that you've chosen to ensure that it's right for you. A few other content management systems that you can explore include Wix or Squarespace. It really depends on the unique needs you deem important for your blog.

The paid way is to buy your own domain name, which will add on a hosting cost as you'll need to pay a hosting company—for example SiteGround—to host or store your website securely. This is relatively inexpensive based on who you choose to host your website. One of the benefits of having your own website is that you're able to use it as a one-stop-shop for all of your passive income avenues. Most if not all of the passive income methods outlined in this book can use your website as a base so it's not a bad idea to invest a little in the beginning to get you started. It is relatively inexpensive and as your passive income methods start to gain traction it will start to pay for itself. Your own domain name can also add to your credibility as an online business owner. If people visit a professional and well put together website they're bound to know, like, and trust you that much more.

Another important requirement for creating a profitable blog is basic knowledge of *search engine optimization (SEO)*. SEO is a tricky concept to get started with if you're coming into blogging completely fresh but once you get the hang of it, it gets easier. SEO helps your blog posts to stay relevant and continue to generate passive income. This is because the keywords that you use in your blog post will help your blog post appear in search engine results when people are searching those keywords. Whenever your blog post comes up and people visit your site, it increases your chances of earning more passive income from your display ads embedded in your blog.

How to Get Started

The key to being able to monetize your blog is choosing a niche that people are interested in and guarantees traffic to your website. A big advantage of having a niche that appeals to your target audience is that they will be searching for information to learn more about this topic. This is where SEO comes in to add a greater lifespan to your blog post, enabling you to continue earning passive income with the help of display ads. If you add other sources of passive income to your blog—such as digital products, online courses or affiliate marketing—SEO will help you continue to make sales and bring in consistent cash flow.

Choose Your Platform

To set up your blog you will need to choose the platform that you want to host it on. Many bloggers prefer WordPress due to its improved SEO functionality. Once you know what platform you're going to use it's important to consider your niche and how you will attract your target audience with content built around your niche subject matter. You need to understand how you can educate, inspire, or entertain your audience to keep them engaged on your blog and coming back to you as an expert in your niche. Understanding how you want to communicate with your target audience on your blog will help you to choose the platform you want to use. For example, WordPress offers many free plugins that will help you to customize your blog to suit the needs of your target audience.

Sort out Your SEO

It's a good idea to understand SEO before you start creating blog content. That way you can ensure that every blog post you write is fully optimized in order to benefit you later when you're able to join an advertising network. The more content that you put on your blog, the greater the chances are that your target audience will find you and increase your blog traffic. Another advantage of creating regular SEO-optimized content is that search engines will determine, based on the solutions you provide in your blog post, whether or not your content is relevant and where to rank your blog.

One of the first places to start when incorporating SEO into your blog posts is to decide on the keywords you'll use in order to attract your target audience. You can conduct keyword research to find out information that will help your blog post rank higher using tools like the *Google Ads Keyword Planner*. You can find out information such as the search volume of particular search terms, as well as related keywords that may add value and increase the chances of your content being found. These keywords can help you to think of blog topics that are more relevant to your target audience to ensure that your blog posts are valuable and can be found by search engines.

Once you know what keywords you're going to focus on in your blog posts you can work on your on-page SEO, which helps search engines understand what your blog post is about in order to show your blog post to those searching for the value you offer. This can be done by incorporating your keywords into your blog post title, URL, headings, the beginning of your blog post, meta-title, meta-description (which is a short blurb sharing what your blog post is about), and the image title, as well as its ALT tag.

An *ALT tag* helps to describe to the search engine what the image that you've used in your blog post depicts. Don't forget to include variations of your keywords or semantic keywords to help your blog post be seen by more people depending on the search terms they use to find your content.

A few other SEO considerations include adding external links within your content that leads to credible sites, adding internal links that link to related pages on your own blog, how long your content is, and whether or not you use multimedia. Multimedia includes elements such as audio or video and can help to increase the amount of time that your target audience spends on your site. Search engines will see your blog as a more credible source if your target audience is engaging with your content for a longer period of time. There is a lot more that can be learned regarding SEO but these are a good start to setting up your blog for success.

Build Your Blog Library

When you're starting your blog, it's crucial to post regular content to keep your blog updated and to start building your content library. Having a content library will help you get into an advertising network. If you apply SEO to each blog post you write you'll see a greater return on your time investment in the future as your content keeps showing up in search engines. Your keyword research can act as a guide to help you decide on what topics you would like to write about, and which of them would be the most relevant to your target audience. You can even use snippets of your blog content on social media to drive traffic back to your blog and increase your chances of making more passive income from your blog.

Join an Advertising Network

Once you have enough blog content and traffic coming to your blog, you can join a credible advertising network such as Google AdSense. An important consideration when placing ads on your site is to determine how you can integrate them more naturally into your content to avoid looking like spam. A few ideas include wrapping the text of your blog post around the ad so that it looks like a natural part of the content, or making sure that banner ads are next to images to help integrate them more.

It's also important to keep in mind ad placement on your blog posts to increase the chance of visitors clicking on the ads. One of the top performing placements is the top left area of your blog content. When you have a good amount of traffic coming to your site and your target audience is engaging with your ads you'll be well on your way to making passive income from your blog! Remember, the work you put in creating blog posts results in continued ad revenue even years after you've published your blog post.

Action Steps

Starting a blog is easy to do, but it can require some effort in the beginning to create enough blog content to qualify for an advertising network. You can however add more passive income streams to your blog in terms of digital products, online courses, affiliate marketing, and even more. If you follow the steps below you will be able to set up your blog successfully.

1. Choose a blogging platform and decide whether you want it to be free or paid.
2. Decide what niche you will blog about and which target audience you will attract.
3. Conduct keyword research to determine blog post topic ideas and optimize your blog.
4. Start writing SEO-optimized blog content to build your content library.
5. Promote your blog posts on social media to increase your traffic.
6. Join an advertising network when you meet their requirements.
7. Receive regular passive income thanks to your SEO-optimized blog posts!

Chapter 3:

Grow Your YouTube Channel

It's very easy to start a YouTube channel, but to be able to monetize your content and start earning passive income it will take much longer. However, there are a few ways to create passive income using YouTube in combination with a few other methods outlined in this book. For example, when your YouTube channel qualifies for AdSense, you will begin to earn ad revenue, you can utilize affiliate marketing, and even include dropshipping, digital products, and online courses—which we'll cover in more detail in later chapters. The work that you put in now to grow your channel will pay off in the long run as it will be easier to maintain with the help of a catalog of evergreen videos that will earn you ad revenue.

How It Works

Creating a YouTube channel is quick, easy and free to do, but growing it will take much longer. However, if you post consistently to your channel, you'll have a greater chance of earning passive income in the future. For example, Ali Abdaal—a YouTuber with almost 3 million subscribers—took six months and 52 videos to qualify for AdSense (2021). Qualifying requires 1,000 subscribers to your channel and 4,000 hours of watch time in the past year. This method is not solely passive, but once you have a library of videos that can be monetized, you'll be able to earn money from them for years to come. Due to the fact that YouTube is owned by Google, it is the second largest search engine, meaning that if your videos are optimized for search terms—similar to that of SEO in blog content—your videos will have a greater chance of showing up in search results on YouTube and Google search results pages.

What You Need

To create YouTube videos, you don't necessarily have to have fancy tech or software. You can easily use your mobile phone or webcam to record videos. Technical know-how is also not a necessity as there is free video editing software you can use; for example DaVinci Resolve, or you can even outsource video editing using freelance websites that are inexpensive such as Upwork. Depending on the type of videos you plan to make you can either script them, have a few talking points written down, or even speak freely if you're knowledgeable enough about the topic. Videos are incredibly popular making them the ideal content format to post online for more engagement with your target audience. Due to their sharable nature, videos are easy to spread online across social media platforms or even to embed into your blog to engage your readers more. Your channel success depends on a few factors on top of channel subscribers or hours of watchtime. You also need to consider how much engagement your videos receive, how popular your niche is, and keep in mind other ways to monetize your YouTube channel for long term success.

How to Get Started

Understanding your niche and target audience is always a crucial step when approaching any passive income endeavor. If you know that people will watch your videos as they cover a topic of interest to them, then you can ensure that your channel will reach the necessary requirements to qualify for AdSense so that you can begin earning passive income from your videos. Once you know what topic your videos will cover and who they will appeal to, you can create and optimize your channel in a manner that will appeal to that audience. When you create videos, it is important to film them with your target audience in mind. Will they find it valuable? Will they watch the whole video or click off early?

Create and Optimize Your Channel

You will need a Google account to create a YouTube channel, and it is often best practice to create a new Gmail email address that is specific to your YouTube channel. That way you can have a unique email address linked to your channel for future business enquiries or audience input. Select a name for your YouTube channel that is reflective of the content you will post that's related to your chosen niche.

At this step it is helpful to search for similar channels in your niche and determine how you can differentiate yourself from them in a way that will appeal to your target audience. If you are posting video content under your own name, try to use your profile picture from your other social media accounts to achieve consistency across platforms. If you are posting video content under a brand name then you can use your logo as your profile picture instead.

The next step is to add information to your channel including a keyword rich description that explains what your channel is about. It can be helpful at this step to do some keyword research based on your niche and target audience to understand what they may be searching in order to find content similar to what you will post on your channel. You can also include links to your website and other social media profiles to help those visiting your channel for the first time understand you a bit better. If you have a blog, linking back to it on your YouTube channel is another great way to drive traffic.

Another feature that you can optimize on your YouTube channel is the cover picture. Many YouTubers share a brief channel introduction—such as who they are and how often they post—on their banner images as well as any call to actions they may have such as subscribing to the channel. Having a fully optimized

YouTube channel means that when people click on your profile they will be more likely to subscribe as they get a clear idea of who you are, which makes for a good first impression.

Record and Upload Regular Videos

The key to creating high quality and engaging YouTube videos is to provide your target audience with entertainment and value that will keep them coming back to your channel. A few ideas for video concepts to get you started include sharing stories that help to educate your target audience about your niche, break down a complicated topic in an entertaining way, or answering commonly asked questions that your target audience would be interested in learning the answers to.

In order to generate interest in your videos, you may need to experiment with different video concepts or formats to determine what works best to attract your target audience. You don't need a lot of technical skill to create these types of videos, although if you want to incorporate graphics or text in your videos that can be done in basic video editing software. You can record videos with your mobile phone or webcam using free recording software like OBS or Audacity. Your audio quality is important to keep in mind to ensure that your videos are clear and easy to understand. It can be useful to purchase an external microphone to ensure optimal audio quality.

Optimizing your videos for search helps to ensure that your audience can find your videos when they're looking for information on your topic. This includes incorporating keywords in your video description and title, creating an eye-catching thumbnail, and a few relevant hashtags. Thumbnails can be easily designed in free design software like Canva. However, the best performing video content is content that adheres to YouTube's ad policies. For example, videos that include sexual content, violence, coarse language, substance abuse, or controversial topics won't qualify for ad revenue, and thus will perform poorly as these videos can be suppressed by the YouTube algorithm. Using copyrighted material is another issue that will negatively impact your videos, for example including popular music in your videos. YouTube does have a library of royalty free music that you can use in your videos instead.

Posting regularly, at least once a week, is important when you're growing your YouTube channel to increase your watchtime and to increase your chances of your content being seen by your target audience. You need to reach 4,000 hours of watchtime on your videos before you can qualify for AdSense, therefore having longer videos can help you to reach those hours faster. Don't try to pad your videos with information that's not of value to your audience just to make longer videos. They will be able to tell, and may not watch the whole video.

One tactic to increase watchtime is to include regular call to actions that ask the viewer to perform some kind of action, for example subscribing to your channel or leaving a comment. Another way to encourage your viewers to watch more videos is to include YouTube cards. These are clickable links that you can use to direct your audience to other videos on your channel that complement what you're talking about. There is also the option to include an endscreen, which is approximately 20 seconds, where you can encourage the viewer to watch related videos or subscribe to the channel.

Encouraging engagement is crucial to the success of your YouTube channel to help grow the number of channel subscribers. Remember to promote your YouTube videos on your other social media platforms or website to increase awareness about your content. YouTube also has the option to create short form videos known as 'shorts'. This is another content format to explore on the platform that may increase your channel reach.

Monetize Your Channel

There are many ways that you can monetize your YouTube channel. This can include AdSense (the most commonly talked about form of monetization), fan funding or channel memberships, affiliate marketing, and merchandising or dropshipping–which will be covered more in Chapter 4.

The amount of passive income you earn from ads can vary greatly as this will depend on your existing library of content as well as new content that you put out. For example, if you look solely at new content created each month, at least once a week, you can make roughly $2 per 1,000 views (Abdaal, 2021). Therefore making money from YouTube isn't completely a passive form of income, but it does offer a convenient work from home opportunity that can turn into a full time job. If you are creating regular content for YouTube another way to generate income is to partner with brands for sponsored branded content. This is not passive but can help to boost your YouTube earnings while you build up a library of evergreen content that will bring in passive income long term.

Once you reach 1,000 subscribers, you can add fan funding to your YouTube earnings through channel memberships. Channel memberships include a monthly fee that your subscribers who opt in would pay to receive exclusive perks and content that's unique to channel members. Again, this is not a completely passive option, but once you get a fair amount of channel members you are able to bring in recurring revenue each month.

It helps to understand the demographics of your subscribers in order to customize content to their needs, for example their gender, age range, location, and their overall engagement with your content. This will inform how you sell to your target audience in terms of adding in other forms of passive income, such as affiliate marketing or dropshipping. If you promote your affiliate links in your video descriptions and within the video content itself, you can increase your chances of viewers clicking on your unique link and making purchases helping you to earn commissions on each sale. Dropshipping and merchandising are other ways to bring in passive income as they are easy to automate and can be a hands off approach to adding extra value to your audience. To generate enough passive income to quit your 9-to-5 job, combining a few complementary methods will increase your chances. A benefit to this is that you will have enough content to help you save time creating other passive income opportunities. For example, if you already have a blog with regular content you can easily create complementary videos to increase your visibility.

Action Steps

It's clear to see that growing a YouTube channel can take time, but the rewards greatly outweigh the negatives. Your videos will be present on the platform for years to come, and if they are correctly optimized for search terms relevant to your niche you can count on ad revenue as a form of passive income.

1. Create and optimize your YouTube channel with keywords related to your niche and target audience.
2. Decide how often you will post and what genre of video you will create.
3. Record your video based on the topic of your niche.
4. Optimize each video you post using keywords in your description, title, hashtags, and tags.
5. Once you're eligible, join the YouTube Partner Program to begin earning ad revenue.
6. Add in other forms of passive income to increase your chances of generating more revenue to ensure long term success.

Chapter 4:

Dropshipping Physical Products

Dropshipping is a more tangible medium to use to generate passive income. The selling point of the dropshipping model is that you can sell physical products without needing to carry your own stock or ship to customers. The wholesaler or distributor that you partner with will take care of all those elements and ship the products to customers under your own label. You don't need to pay for the product out of pocket as that cost is covered by the customer. It does take hard work to get dropshipping set up and running smoothly, but once you've selected the right distributor, you can save time and automate the process. There is less risk involved as you can test various dropshipping products your target audience wants with little money.

How It Works

The biggest benefit to dropshipping is that you don't need to purchase the products you want to sell beforehand. This gives you more leeway to sell a variety of products without carrying stock. You won't need to store stock in warehouses, as the distributor will carry stock and send it straight from their own warehouse. The distributor will also take care of packing and shipping product orders, as well as dealing with any returns that customers may make. You also won't need to worry about keeping inventory of stock or ordering more products. Dropshipping is one of the easiest ways to break into the ecommerce space without needing to spend money on stock.

What You Need

All you need to begin dropshipping is an internet connection and a few low cost expenses, such as website hosting and a domain name. The costs may increase as your online store grows, but it will still work out less than creating and selling your own physical products. Dropshipping will take place on your own website as you would sell the products under your name. This is easy to do with ecommerce software like *Shopify*.

Shopify has an app called *DSers* that will assist you with selecting products to sell on your own online store. Using this app you can quickly and easily import the products you want to sell from *AliExpress* onto your own website. When a visitor to your site purchases one of the products you've selected to sell the DSer app will fulfill this order automatically. The supplier from AliExpress will then send the product to the customer on your behalf. It's important to test this process yourself to ensure that elements such as the labeling of packages and invoices look consistent with your brand– and that the products themselves arrive in good condition! Although your orders are fulfilled by the distributor, any customer complaints will be directed at you.

How to Get Started

Dropshipping is easy to get started with as it can be an automated process with less admin than a brick and mortar store. It does differ from a model, such as print on demand, as you have less control over product customization. Instead, you will select products from a catalog that you can sell on your own store. There is the potential to earn more via dropshipping versus affiliate marketing as you will be selling your own products at your own markup. However, both dropshipping and affiliate marketing can complement one another and offer your target audience more options that will suit their needs.

Market and Product Research

To begin dropshipping as a form of passive income, it's important to understand what products are relevant to your niche. If the products are unrelated, they likely won't appeal to your target audience, making them more difficult to sell. Conducting market research will help as you can get a clearer idea of the kinds of products your target audience would be interested in buying. For example, if you're in the fitness niche it would make more sense to sell activewear as opposed to furniture.

Having niche products can also work in your favor as you can become known as the go-to supplier of these products. It may also depend on what products wholesalers or distributors have available for purchase. Here you may need to do product research to decide what products you want to offer centered around what your target audience needs and wants. If you can address their needs and ensure that the products you choose are of a high quality, then you should have strong foundations in place to begin dropshipping as part of your passive income stream. Uncovering these needs can be done with the help of websites like Google and Answer the Public to find keywords that your target audience may be searching. Online stores, for example Amazon or eBay, can help you to find trending and popular products that are likely to sell.

One thing to keep in mind is that dropshipping distributors may have higher prices than ordinary wholesalers, which would make it difficult to have competitive prices in your niche market. Here it becomes important to really take the time to conduct proper research and test the products yourself before opening your online store. This can take time and costs may vary depending on the products you want to sell but it will benefit you in the long run as you are more likely to have satisfied customers and less returns. Consumers will compare prices and if your price is too high in comparison to other stores–even if their quality is not as good–you may not be able to make as many sales. Keep this in mind when settling on a retail price for customers and do a bit of research into your competitors' prices.

You can differentiate yourself further and limit competition if you sell products that may be hard for your target audience to find in their area. If you can offer them the convenience of getting the product they're looking for delivered straight to their door, you have a better chance of making that sale when your target audience is searching for that product. Another way to add value to your online store is to offer complementary items or accessories to your higher priced product offerings. By including these accessories you can increase your chances of your target audience purchasing more from your online store. Remember that smaller items may sell better due to lower shipping costs.

Set Up Your Store

There are a few options to consider when setting up your dropshipping store: You can choose Shopify as your ecommerce software combined with the DSers app, or you could host it on your own website, for example WordPress, with the help of wholesaler or distributor directories. WorldWide Brands and WholeSale Central are two options that you can explore to find products you can sell through dropshipping. There are a few key players to keep in mind when understanding the process of dropshipping. The manufacturers create the products and send them to the wholesalers who will sell them at a wholesale price. You as the dropshipper will select your wholesale products at wholesale prices and add your own markup to create the retail price that you will list on your online store. Customers will pay the retail price that you list ensuring that you can make a profit based on your markup. When the customer places their order you'll need to let the wholesaler know and the product will be sent directly to the customer without the need for you to get involved. As mentioned, this process can be automated to help generate passive income with minimal involvement.

In order to be able to engage with wholesalers you will need to register your business and follow tax regulations specific to your area. This can add complexities to dropshipping as a passive income method, but if you want to grow your online store to sell a range of products that will benefit your target audience, it will be worth it in the end. The dropshipping model also allows for growth as you'll have less costs to worry about and less work to do since the automated process should run smoothly in the background. The convenience and flexibility that dropshipping offers you makes it the ideal way to operate your own online store at home without the need to worry about stock or storage. However, you will need to differentiate your store from competitors that depend on low prices to appear more attractive to consumers.

SEO can help you here if you optimize your online store with keywords that will appeal to your target audience and address their needs when they're searching for those terms. If you can position yourself as an authority in your niche you may have a better chance at converting customers with your online store.

Promote Your Products

You have no control over the product and how it may look or function, due to it being sourced from wholesalers who receive the products from the manufacturers. You will face more competition as other dropshippers will be selling similar, if not the same, products. This is where marketing and promoting your products comes in as you will have control over the message you share with your target audience. If you can find many different ways to market your products you'll have an easier time selling them. Doing competitor research by looking at the top ranking websites that sell products similar to you can help you determine how to position your products strongly on your website and in your marketing material. You should put a lot of your focus on optimizing your online store for search engines, generating traffic to your online store, and actively marketing your products.

To succeed in marketing your products and your online store you will need to have an attractive *value proposition* that sets you apart from competitors. Your unique value proposition should help your customers understand why they should buy your product and how you can fulfill their individual needs.

A few ideas to help you craft your value proposition include examining the benefits your products offer as well as the problem it solves. Other factors such as price and quality can also factor into your value proposition. Once you have a solid value proposition in place, you can begin to explore how you can reach your target audience with your message. Considering their demographics, interests, and behavior will help you to craft a marketing message that speaks directly to your customer, and encourages them to buy your product as it will be aligned with their core values. With a powerful marketing message, you can begin to attract your target audience in various ways such as content marketing– this is where your blog or YouTube channel could come into play. Some other options include online advertising on social media or search engines— although this may incur extra costs, and influencer marketing through collaborations or communities.

Building a know, like, and trust factor around your online store is important to increase conversions and sales. If you add certain customer-focused elements to your store such as reviews or money back guarantees you can increase trust with your target audience as they will appreciate your transparency.

Action Steps

The sooner you can get your online store up and running and begin selling products through dropshipping, the sooner you can start earning passive income. Taking these steps to build a successful online business from home can offer you more freedom and build your authority online should you wish to add on other passive income avenues.

1. Understand your target audience and their needs.
2. Research which products relevant to your niche can fulfill these needs.
3. Decide on a wholesaler or a few wholesalers you will purchase these products from.
4. Set up your online store using, for example, Shopify and DSers to begin dropshipping.
5. Ensure that you have the capacity to offer customer service should you need to—this can be outsourced if you have the budget.
6. Start promoting your products with your unique value proposition!

Chapter 5:

Attractive Digital Products That Sell

Digital products are an easy and inexpensive way to get started with making passive income online, as you don't need a lot of technical knowledge to create them. They are delivered virtually meaning that you have no production or shipping costs. Digital products can include ebooks, photos, templates, audiobooks, software, illustrations, online courses—although we'll go into more detail about online courses in the next chapter—and more. Ebooks, for example, are an excellent entry-level digital product because you can turn your existing knowledge into a valuable product for potential customers.

How It Works

There are few steps to follow when creating your first digital product. You come up with an innovative product concept, create the digital product in the format you choose, place it on a marketplace or your own online store to sell, and promote it to drive sales.

You have two options regarding where you can sell your digital products: You can either sell them on your own website with a higher profit margin, as you're not relying on other marketplaces; or you can sell your digital products on marketplaces like Sellfy, Amazon or Ebay.

The advantages of using platforms such as Sellfy are that they receive a lot of traffic and you may have an easier time driving sales. Selling digital products on your own website might take a little longer and depend on you promoting them or even running ads to draw attention to them. However, once you've created the product and set up your online store or marketplace, you can continue to sell that product on repeat to generate passive income.

What You Need

When selling digital products, there are a few key pieces that you need to have in place before you can guarantee sales. Of course, making the product itself and determining where you would like to sell it are important factors, but another consideration is having an email list of engaged buyers. If you're completely new to online business an email list is a more personal way of engaging with your audience that you may have accumulated on social media. An email list can be helpful regarding all passive income avenues but it's particularly useful when selling digital products as you can directly link to your products and share a more meaningful message with your recipients. Growing an email list may take time but there are ways to get a headstart that will lead your audience to your digital product.

How to Get Started

Whatever your skill level or interests may be, there is certainly a way to package that up into a digital product that you can sell. Make a list of all the ideas you have related to your subject matter that you know people can benefit from. These topics will be excellent content for your digital product as it will cover what many people don't know and help them to correct any mistakes or misconceptions they have about the topic. Remember, the knowledge that you have will be valuable to someone else, and by creating a digital product you're able to share that knowledge with them and generate sales. Before you create your digital product, it's a good idea to do some research to validate your idea and make sure that it is something people would be willing to spend money on. Plus, having a better idea of your target audience and niche will help you determine where you should be selling your product.

Product Research

In Chapter 1 we went into more detail about how to identify your niche and target audience. These two factors will help you to decide what genre or form your digital product will take. Your niche will guide you on the subject matter of your digital product, while your target audience will help you to decide on how you will present the information you share in your digital product. For example, if your niche is fitness and your target audience is busy moms, your digital product could be an audiobook that busy moms can listen to on their way to pick up their kids from school.

The next step is to research whether or not your product idea will be a profitable venture. Doing research on what product you can create doesn't need to be a time consuming process. There is a quick and easy way to decide whether or not a product is worth creating. If you search your product idea on a marketplace such as Amazon, you should be able to see a collection of search results. By taking a look at the number of results that come back, you'll know that your product idea is worth selling as there is already a demand for it. If there are no results, it may be a good idea to alter your digital product idea to one that has more search traffic.

Once you have validated your digital product idea, the next step is to look for a gap that you can fill. Can you see any product ideas that are missing from your search results that you feel would be valuable for your target audience? Perhaps you can sort through reviews and see what customers in your target audience are saying they need on related popular products. Once you're able to identify a gap that your digital product can fill, you'll have a validated product idea that will stand out from the rest.

Create Your Digital Product

In order to create a digital product that sells, you need to make sure that you're helping your target audience reach a goal that holds a lot of meaning to them. That way you can take your product research and create a product that focuses on that core topic, and on how your target audience can achieve results that will take them closer to reaching their goal.

Depending on what type of product you decide to make, the tech you need will differ. An ebook is an easy starting point as you can use a simple document to type your book and easily publish to Amazon or even share the PDF document on your own website for customers to purchase. If you decide to go with Amazon self-publishing, you can use their free *Kindle Direct Publishing (KDP)* platform, and the Kindle Create formatting application. KDP allows you to publish your book quickly and easily letting you reach more people due to the worldwide presence that Amazon has online. Kindle Create is an application you can use to format your ebook for different mediums on Amazon. Once your book is written and ready to publish, you will need to include an eye-catching title and cover page, plus an enticing book description to encourage readers to buy. Keep in mind that ebooks of approximately 10,000 to 15,000 words on Amazon cost between $0.99 and $2.99. However, if you're looking to earn more royalties, it is recommended to price your ebooks in the range of $2.99 to $9.99.

You can easily turn your ebook into an audiobook by recording yourself reading the book with a simple app on your phone. The next chapter will go into more detail about online courses, which will help you understand how to create digital products that incorporate video. When creating your first digital product, it's a good idea to focus on one topic at a time. This makes it easier for your target audience to understand and allows you room to grow your digital product suite. However, once established, you will need to grow that audience.

Diversify Your Product Suite

Diversifying your product offering is a crucial step to reaching more people with your digital products and ensuring a greater chance of earning passive income. This means that you would create a few digital products around your niche topic that are in different formats to attract different people. It is a good idea to have a variety of offer formats that reach each type of learner: kinesthetic, visual, and auditory. For example, if you create a pre-recorded masterclass it will appeal to a visual learner whereas if you add an audiobook to your product suite you will attract an auditory learner. Which type of learner would you like to appeal to? One way to decide on which learning style to select is to think about the lifestyle that your ideal client lives. Do they have enough time to watch a masterclass series? Don't overlook audio content as many people enjoy listening to audiobooks on-the-go over reading.

When diversifying your product range, it's important to consider the price points of your digital products. You should aim to have a low-priced entry-level product, which leads to a mid-level product, and finally to a higher-ticket product. This allows a range of customers to purchase your products, as they will each be on different "customer journeys" and have a particular budget that they can spend on your digital products.

The Customer Journey

A "customer journey" refers to how you take your ideal audience from point A to point B in order to purchase your digital product. It also increases your chances of retaining customers as if they purchase your entry-level product, and they enjoy it they may purchase your mid-level product, and so on. You'll be able to earn more passive income this way and once your products are up and running this process can easily be automated for less work from your side. Remember to link these products back to the goals that your target audience have so that they can see how your digital products will be of benefit to them. A huge advantage to having this product suite in place means that each product will guide your customer through the journey, which minimizes some of the marketing activities you'll need to implement as the products will practically sell themselves! If your entry-level digital product is attractive enough, your target audience will purchase it and be moved through your customer journey.

Marketplaces Versus Your Own Website

There are many places to sell your digital products. An easy starting point for beginners would be to focus on digital marketplaces like Amazon or Sellfy. Digital marketplaces do everything for you as they have all of the tech as well as an audience ready to buy. It's an easy sign-up process to join a digital marketplace, however it's important to keep in mind that most marketplaces will take a percentage of your profits through commissions on each sale you make. Due to the large amount of products available on digital marketplaces, it's imperative that your digital products stand out amongst the rest. You can upload your digital products to multiple digital marketplaces if you would like to increase your chances of earning passive income on these platforms.

Shopify is a popular ecommerce software that can help you to quickly set up your own online store. The basic plan is $29 per month, meaning that there is an upfront investment to creating your own store. Although Shopify creates an easy to use online store, it is not able to host your digital products. It does have an additional app that you'll need to install in order to sell digital products. The *Downloadable Digital Assets* app is free to install and its starter package is $5 per month. This is a good option to go for if you would like to have your own store front that's simple to use.

Another option is using your own website to host and sell your digital products. If you have a WordPress blog you can add an ecommerce plugin such as WooCommerce to sell your digital products. This option is a little more complicated as you'll need a payment gateway such as Stripe or Paypal to accept payments. There are also many different extensions that you can select to enhance your online store functionality. It may be a little more complicated but it can offer you flexibility and customization. WooCommerce is a free WordPress plugin, although you will have your domain name and hosting costs to consider. For a more all-in-one website platform SquareSpace is another option. The professional plan is $23 per month but it includes ecommerce functionality, a domain, and hosting.

It depends on how much customization you need as well as your budget to select a marketplace versus your own website. Marketplaces have the bonus of doing most of the marketing for you as they have an existing audience. If you choose to sell your digital products on your own website, you may need to do marketing for yourself including ads or growing your own audience.

Creating a Ready-To-Buy Audience

In terms of creating digital products one of the most effective means of earning passive income is through email marketing. Email marketing involves building an email list of members in your target audience that opt in to receive email marketing material from you—typically informational newsletters. To encourage sign-ups to your newsletter or email marketing efforts, it's important to have a *landing page*. A landing page can be created in your email marketing software—such as Mailchimp or Mailerlite—or on your website to collect email addresses. Both Mailchimp and Mailerlite have free plans that you can use when starting out.

In order to get your target audience interested in joining your email list, it helps to have a free resource that they can receive as an incentive. This could be as simple as a checklist or cheat sheet created in a simple one-page PDF that your target audience can download. Once they're on your email list, you can start building a relationship with them by offering value and leading them into your customer journey with your low-ticket digital product. The more you grow your email list the more potential customers you can share your digital products with to generate passive income. This can take some time and effort in the beginning, but once you grow your email list and start making sales, it will start to grow itself further. You can invest in social media advertising if you want to speed up the process, but that can come later, once you're making passive income to break even.

Action Steps

With the creation of your entry-level digital product and a way to sell to your email list, you can start generating passive income!

1. Do product research to make sure that your product idea is profitable and speaks to your target audience.
2. Create your entry-level digital product to start promoting.
3. Select a marketplace to sign-up for or set up your website to start selling.
4. Grow your email list to sell your digital products or invest in ads.

5. Begin to diversify your digital product offering to add complementary digital products.
6. Make passive income from your digital product funnel!

Chapter 6:

Create Your Own Course

Creating your own online course can be a more profitable passive income route to take. As opposed to digital download products, such as ebooks, they are a little more labor intensive—meaning that you can charge more for them. If you create a $9.99 ebook, you can potentially sell your online course covering a similar topic for $149. There are a few platform considerations to keep in mind, for example if you choose to host your online course on a platform like Udemy, you won't have as much flexibility in terms of pricing your course.

How It Works

Similar to creating a digital product you are using your existing knowledge (or learned knowledge) to create a product that you can sell. An online course is more engaging and can appeal to a wide range of learners as you can include a variety of learning elements such as text, video, and audio content. As with previous passive income avenues we've covered so far, you will need to find what your target audience is looking for and will actually pay for. You can do this by doing a bit of market research. There are a few ways to conduct market research in order to determine what your target audience needs and—most importantly—wants. You can ask your target audience what they want to learn either through the use of a questionnaire, interviews, or simply social media. You can also browse other courses that are in your niche to identify a knowledge gap. When researching similar courses that may be competing with your own, be sure to read reviews to understand what gaps you can address in your own course material.

It's helpful to outline the course subject matter once you've chosen your topic in order to get feedback from others before you spend time creating it. If you can get feedback from someone in your target audience, this can help to validate your idea and ensure that it will sell. Try asking someone who is not as knowledgeable in the subject matter of your course but has interest in learning in order to find out whether your course outline is easy to understand and clear enough. Online courses are more time intensive, but there are a few different methods you can choose to create one that may speak more to your skill level and expertise. Once your course is created there are a range of ways to start selling it to your target audience. You can list it on course marketplaces like Udemy, use course specific platforms such as Kajabi, or create a course on your own website using a plugin like LearnDash on WordPress. When your course is created and ready to buy, you can start promoting it to drive sales.

How to Get Started

Compared to the other passive income methods outlined in this book, creating an online course is a little more work, but incredibly rewarding. There are many factors to consider before getting started to ensure that you're able to create your course and continue to sell it. If the course creation process is rushed, you may need to redo sections, which will take up more time and resources. If you have other passive income avenues already running—for example, a few digital products on sale—you'll be able to spend a bit more time creating your course, as you will already be earning passive income in the meantime. The added benefit to having other content already available is that you can use some of that existing content—whether it be blog posts, YouTube videos, or even an ebook—to create the outline or base for your course. This will save you a lot of time and resources instead of having to create your course from scratch.

Creating Your Course

The very first step to creating your course is to understand your target audience and niche thoroughly. Having a clear picture of your target audience in mind will allow you to understand what they need to learn and what from your niche is relevant to them. It's important to strike a balance between giving them all of the information and giving them only the information they need to reach their goal. You as the expert may feel that they need to know everything you know, but the truth is that this will only overwhelm them. Focus on what they need to know now to help them reach their desired transformation. A benefit to developing your course in this way is that it gives you room to create more courses later on to increase your passive income stream. Remember to validate your course idea based on similar topic searches on course platforms such as Udemy. By addressing a knowledge gap within those marketplaces you will be able to refine your course idea and ensure that your target audience is interested enough to invest in your course.

Developing learning objectives for your course can be an invaluable step, as you can clearly map out what it is that your students need to learn. This forms the base of your course because you'll be able to determine what content you need to include to ensure that your target audience will reach these objectives. With these learning objectives in mind, you can begin to structure your content to create a solid outline to help you build your course.

Including activities or tasks within your course outline can help to increase the engagement that your students will have with your course material. Once your course outline has been created with your target audience, niche, and learning objectives in mind, you can start to create the material that your students will engage with. You may need to conduct further research into your topic to make sure that you're covering all the core points that your students will need to learn. The length of time this takes will be dependent on your existing knowledge, however it is always good to include practical examples or facts to help substantiate your own teachings and add credibility to your course. Your target audience will be made up of different types of learners, which we touched on earlier, so try to include a few differently created resources to retain their interest. These could be videos, audio bites, worksheets, and more.

Video is the most popular medium when it comes to creating an online course, although including written resources—for example worksheets—to complement your videos can add extra value and engage your students further. One method is to create a collection of slides that you can take the student through using voiceover. It's a simple method that can be done for free in software like PowerPoint or Canva. This voiceover method can be enhanced by including your face in a small section of the screen—all you need is a webcam to record yourself talking through the slides. Keep audio quality in mind as you need to be clear and easy to understand. Depending on your existing tech you may need to invest in a microphone. If your topic is not suited to slides, or is more practical in nature, you can film yourself doing a demonstration with your webcam, mobile phone, or camera.

Another option is to emulate a lecture by using a whiteboard to write down key points to help educate your students. In this case it can be helpful to prepare a script or a few bullet points that you can use to guide your lesson. It's best to keep your lessons at maximum 20 minutes to avoid overwhelming your students and to help you keep your lesson clear and concise. Using your existing tech can help you to save money when creating a course, but if you need to upgrade your equipment, for example your camera, you may end up spending more.

There are a few notes to keep in mind when it comes to the tech you need to create your course and the skill level that may be needed to utilize this tech. You may be able to use the existing tech that you have access to, but if you want your course quality to match those of other course creators, you may need to invest a bit more money. However, a good quality camera and microphone aren't the only considerations. If you are creating a few videos for your course you may need to edit them in software such as Adobe Premiere Pro. Video editing software varies in price and you can certainly spend time teaching yourself how to use it, but if you want to get your course out to start earning passive income as soon as possible, you may need to outsource it. It is easy to find affordable professionals on websites such as Upwork or Freelancer. You can even find freelancers to help you script and create course material too if you need more help.

If your course subject matter is likely to change due to industry news—for example social media algorithm updates—it will be to your benefit to keep your course updated. Having an up to date course means that it will still be relevant to your target audience years later and continue bringing in passive income. Learning new skills can be challenging for people so ensuring that your course is up to date, well-structured, and comprehensive will improve your chances of making more course sales. However, keep in mind that depending on where you host your course your passive income will vary.

Where to Host Your Course

Where you decide to host your course will be dependent on your skill level and the resources you have available such as your budget or time restraints. The easiest option to start with is placing your course onto a course marketplace, for example Udemy or Skillshare. Course marketplaces such as these have courses that span many different skill levels meaning that you can create an entry-level course or a more advanced course. If you keep your product suite in mind, you could potentially create a few courses that take your target audience from the beginning, middle, and finally to the end thereby increasing your chances of earning more passive income.

Listing your course on Udemy does have some cons as there are a few requirements you will need to meet. For example, they specify the minimum number of minutes your video may be, there is an extensive review process, and due to the many discounts that Udemy offers to appeal to more customers, you may not be able to sell your course for as much as you would like. Udemy also takes a percentage of sales in exchange for listing your course on their platform. One of the benefits to hosting your course on a platform like Udemy is that people are coming to their site to specifically look for courses. If your course is optimized and covers a topic people want to learn about, you will have a better chance of more people seeing and purchasing your course. The people that purchase from Udemy are usually looking for courses that are more practical in nature that will help them to improve or learn new skills that will benefit them in the workplace. Keeping this in mind will help you to tailor your courses to these consumer needs.

Although course marketplaces offer convenience, there is the downside in terms of what you can charge for your course. Therefore, if you are looking to have more control over your course and how you deliver it, you can choose a course specific platform or create course functionality on your existing website. An example of a course platform is Kajabi, which offers an all-in-one solution to creating, selling, and promoting your online course. It is an expensive option with the basic plan being $119 per month if billed annually, however it does include email marketing, a website, funnel building, and more that can replace your need for a separate website or email marketing software.

If you have an existing website, you can incorporate course software to host your own courses. For example, WordPress has many learning management system plugins including LearnDash. Although hosting your course on your own website has many benefits—for example, you have more control over your course content and delivery—WordPress and LearnDash do require more technical knowledge. If you are familiar with WordPress you should be able to manage, otherwise a WordPress developer may need to be hired to assist you. Due to the fact that online courses are more complex than downloadable digital products, you may need to consider having customer service to assist customers if they have any issues with course access.

If Kajabi or LearnDash are out of your budget, another option that includes slightly less tech would be to create an email course. This is a text-only course that would be delivered via your email marketing platform, for example Mailchimp. You would set up an email automation that would ensure students who purchase your course receive their emails with learning material included every day or week for as long as the course runs. It may not be as engaging as a video course, but if you want to test your course first before investing in software like Kajabi, it could be an option to consider.

Marketing Your Course

After you've created your course and set it up using your platform of choice, you will need to market it in various ways depending on the platform you choose. Spend time creating a course title that speaks to the benefits that your course will offer your target audience. An enticing course title will be easier to sell than one that is vague or doesn't offer your target audience a big enough transformation.

Udemy makes marketing your course easy because they have promotion programs that are personalized to their users. On the other hand, Kajabi or WordPress hosted courses are reliant on your efforts to get your target audience to purchase your course. This means that you would need to focus on promoting your course using social media, email marketing, SEO, or ads to reach more people in your target audience. One method would be to create a landing page on your website that directs people to your online course. This gives you the opportunity to use SEO to optimize your landing page and offers you a shareable link that you can promote on other platforms. If you have influential peers in your space you could even approach them with a sneak peek of your course to get them to promote it on your behalf thus widening your reach. The more places you can share about your course the better!

On Udemy you have the option to make your course free. This may seem counterproductive when the aim is to earn passive income, but by having a free course available that adds value to your target audience will grow your know, like, and trust factor on the platform. If you are able to get good reviews on your free course, you will increase your chances of having more sign-ups to your paid courses. This tactic can help to build your product suite as your free course draws your target audience into your customer journey. Once they are part of your customer journey you can begin promoting other courses or complementary digital products to increase your earnings.

An often overlooked option is creating a membership centered around your online course to bring in monthly recurring revenue. This could be as simple as offering a private discussion forum where you share updates to your course or complementary resources. It adds an extra selling point to your course and doesn't require much effort on your part to maintain. If you sell your course plus a monthly membership on top of that. you can increase your chances of earning more passive income. If you're looking to bring in passive income sooner using online courses you can 'presell' your course. 'Preselling' means that you sell your course before you even start making it, which can be an excellent way to validate your course idea and bring in enough money to invest in equipment or professionals to create your course.

Actions Steps

There are many different ways to create a course, but if you do your research and outline from the beginning you will be able to save time and resources.

1. Find out what your target audience wants to learn about, related to your niche, through market research.
2. Based on the knowledge gap you find, create your course outline, including learning objectives.
3. Decide on the format your course will take, for example videos with slides or videos demonstrating something.
4. Select a course platform, such as Udemy, Kajabi, or WordPress, where you will publish your course.
5. Start marketing your course and earning passive income.

Conclusion

Generating enough passive income to quit your 9-to-5 does take time. In this book we've outlined six potential ways to earn passive income, but each comes with their own pros and cons. Some may involve more technical knowledge than others, and expenses can differ too. However, once the hard work is done and all the steps have been followed to successfully set up one or a combination of these passive income streams, you will benefit long term with minimal upkeep.

Affiliate marketing is an easy option as you don't need to create anything, but rather focus on selling other businesses' products or services. You do need to have an engaged audience that will buy these products using your unique link though. Growing an audience can take time but once you have a sizable email list or a large number of social media followers you will be able to earn a fair amount of passive income from these sales. Affiliate marketing can be paired perfectly with the other methods mentioned in this book—particularly a blog and/or YouTube channel to expand your reach and influence to encourage more affiliate sales.

The content that you create on your blog or on YouTube can be repurposed into other forms of passive income such as digital products or online courses. Repackaging your knowledge of your niche with the needs of your target audience in mind will help you to create a profitable product suite that you can automate and sell on repeat. As your online business grows you can add more digital products or courses to continue growing your passive income.

There is no cap to your earnings like there is with a 9-to-5 full time job. If you put in the initial work to follow the steps outlined in this book in order to set up these passive income streams, you'll be able to take your time back to spend on family, friends, and hobbies.

This is by no means an exhaustive list of all the possible ways to generate passive income, but these methods are inexpensive and require little technical knowledge to set up. By combining these options—potentially all six of them—you will increase your chances of generating enough passive income to quit your full time job and focus on achieving time freedom as these processes run in the background. Each method will involve maintenance, such as posting YouTube videos or writing blog posts, but once you begin earning money from each, the content you create now will continue to work for you in the future.

It is up to you to decide what to try first and which combinations to try. The key to each is growing an audience that will engage with your methods of passive income. If you begin growing your audience today you will be able to get a headstart on these passive income methods, as you'll have an audience primed and ready to either buy from you or interact with ads to assist you in earning passive income from ad revenue. Don't underestimate the power of social media, and a solid email list to help you generate passive income. The sooner you get started, the sooner you can start benefiting from the opportunities that passive income has to offer. So go on, make an investment in yourself; you've got work to do.

References

Abdaal, A. (2021, April 15). *9 passive income ideas - how i make $27k per week* [Video]. YouTube. https://www.youtube.com/watch?v=M5y69v1RbU0

Amazon Associates. (n.d.). *Amazon associates - Amazon's affiliate marketing program.* Amazon. https://affiliate-program.amazon.com/

Ferreira, C. (2022, January 13). *What is dropshipping?* Shopify. https://www.shopify.co.za/blog/what-is-dropshipping

Harrison, B. (2014). *Passive income secrets: The essential how-to guide for creating financial freedom and living the life you have always wanted!* PDFdrive.com. https://www.pdfdrive.com/passive-income-secrets-the-essential-how-to-guide-for-creating-financial-freedom-and-living-the-life-you-have-always-wanted-e194980556.html

Juviler, J. (2020, October 6). *7 ways to monetize your Wordpress blog.* HubSpot. https://blog.hubspot.com/website/how-to-monetize-wordpress

Kajabi. (n.d.). *Pricing.* https://kajabi.com/pricing

Kumar, B. (2022, February 18). *How to make money on youtube in 2022.* Shopify.

https://www.shopify.co.za/blog/198134793-how-to-make-money-on-youtube

Lee, J. (2021, March 18). *Affiliate marketing for beginners: What you need to know.* HubSpot. https://blog.hubspot.com/marketing/affiliate-marketing-guide

Mardan, A. (2018). *Using your web skills to make money.* PDFdrive.com. https://www.pdfdrive.com/using-your-web-skills-to-make-money-secrets-of-a-successful-online-course-creator-and-other-income-strategies-that-really-work-e158342668.html

Oetting, J. (2021, November 30). *The ultimate guide to seo in 2022.* HubSpot. https://blog.hubspot.com/marketing/seo

Olsson, M. (n.d.). *Build a profitable online business: the no-nonsense guide.* PDFdrive.com. https://www.pdfdrive.com/build-a-profitable-online-business-the-no-nonsense-guide-e157689463.html

Penn, J. (2015). *How to make a living with your writing: Books, blogging and more.* PDFdrive.com. https://www.pdfdrive.com/how-to-make-a-living-with-your-writing-books-blogging-and-more-e158952970.html

Puffin, J. (2015). *The critical guide to passive income.* PDFdrive.com. https://www.pdfdrive.com/the-critical-guide-to-passive-income-a-thorough-exploration-e194983930.html

Shopify. (n.d.). *Pricing.* https://www.shopify.co.za/pricing

Squarespace. (n.d.). *Pricing.* https://www.squarespace.com/pricing

Udemy Teaching Center. (n.d.). *Recommended course creation process.* Udemy. https://teach.udemy.com/course-creation/recommended-course-creation-process/

Waters, R. (n.d.). *Passive income: Your complete guide to building multiple streams of passive income.* PDFdrive.com. https://www.pdfdrive.com/passive-income-stop-working-start-living-make-money-while-you-sleep-e199657613.html

Wolf, S. (2016). *Passive income: develop a passive income empire: Complete beginners guide to building riches through multiple streams.* PDFdrive.com. https://www.pdfdrive.com/passive-income-develop-a-passive-income-empire-complete-beginners-guide-to-building-riches-e200445491.html

YouTube Help. (n.d.). *How to earn money on youtube.* Google. https://support.google.com/youtube/answer/72857?hl=en

Printed in Great Britain
by Amazon